What You Wanna Know

What You Wanna Know:

BACKSTREET

St. Martin's Griffin ✖ New York

BOYS

Secrets Only a Girlfriend Can Tell

Samantha Stonebraker

In loving memory of my Aunt Elsie,
and my three best friends,
Steven, John, and Mari.
I love you.

♥

Library of Congress Cataloging-in-Publication Data

ISBN 0-312-26114-4

First St. Martin's Griffin Edition: November 1999

10 9 8 7 6 5 4 3 2 1

acknowledgments

Taking on a project like this requires a lot of motivation and support. It has definitely been a team effort and there are so many people that I must thank. First I must give a shout out to the the Backstreet Boys because without them I wouldn't have these groovy experiences to write about. Hey Brian, 7272333 (back at you LOL). My parents, Garry and Teri, for your everlasting love and support, you are my inspiration. Steven, John, and Mari for being my laughter even when "big sis" was down, I love you guys. The cool girls that kept me in tune to what you wanted to know about the BSB, especially Jena, Rachel, and Kelly—thanks. My girls, Kelley, Katie, Laura, and Shannon, what would I do without friends like you! Giles Anderson at the Scott Waxman Agency for believing in my project. Joe Veltre and Erika Fad at St. Martin's for all your work and support. Last, but definitely not least, my love, Stephen Thomas! You've been the missing piece to my puzzle, you're hip, you're cool (do you hear my nose). Everyone else, I'm new at this so know that you have my love and appreciation. And I'm spent.

contents

[1] How did you and Brian meet?   1

[2] What were some romantic things Brian did for you?   2

[3] Do the Backstreet Boys wear boxers or briefs? Who looks the best in them?   4

[4] What do the Boys do before one of their concerts?   6

[5] What was the prom like with Brian?   8

[6] Do any of the Backstreet Boys drink alcohol or take drugs?   10

[7] Do any of the Backstreet Boys have girlfriends?   12

[8] What do Brian and the Backstreet Boys enjoy doing when they aren't performing? What do they do in their spare time?   14

[9] Were you ever with Brian when he encountered his biggest fear?   16

[10] How have the Backstreet Boys changed because of their success?   18

[11] What was the funniest moment you shared with the Backstreet Boys?   20

[12] How do Brian and his loved ones cope with his heart condition?   22

[13] What are Brian's favorite foods? What are the special recipes that he likes the most?   24

[14] Were you ever around when the Backstreet Boys filmed their videos? What were they like?   26

[15] Do the Backstreet Boys ever wear makeup?   28

[16] Is Brian a good kisser?   30

[17] Were there ever any hard times with the Backstreet Boys?   32

[18] What was it like being a girlfriend of one of the Backstreet Boys? How did you get along with the other members?   34

[19] Was Brian really bitten by a spider?   36

[20] What is Brian most sensitive about?   38

[21] What was it like going home with Brian to Kentucky?   40

[22] Did you go to the same high school as any of the Backstreet Boys?   42

[23] What was the best trip you took with the Backstreet Boys?   44

[24] How do the Backstreet Boys get along?   46

[25] Tell us a good story about the Backstreet Boys before they were famous.   **48**

[26] What were the parties like at Lou Pearlman's house?   **50**

[27] Did Brian ever do anything to make you mad?   **52**

[28] What was a typical date like with Brian? Did you ever double-date with other members of the Backstreet Boys?   **54**

[29] Are any of the Backstreet Boys virgins?   **56**

[30] What do Brian and the Backstreet Boys like most about fans? What do they hate about them?   **58**

[31] Do the Backstreet Boys lip-sync in concert?   **60**

[32] How do the Backstreet Boys feel about all the other boy groups that are popular right now?   **62**

[33] What is Brian's biggest secret?   **64**

[34] How do the Backstreet Boys celebrate their birthdays?   **66**

[35] How can a fan meet the Backstreet Boys?   **68**

[36] What was Brian's biggest surprise for you?   **70**

[37] How long did you tour with the Backstreet Boys? What was it like from day to day?   **72**

[38] What kind of clothes do Brian and the other Backstreet Boys like their girlfriends to wear?   **74**

[39] Do you wish you could have dated one of the other Backstreet Boys? How did the other members treat their girlfriends?   **76**

[40] What is the most outrageous thing you ever saw a fan do?   **78**

[41] How can a fan break into the music business?   **80**

[42] Did you and Brian ever have a pet together?   **82**

[43] What music inspired Brian and the Boys?   **84**

[44] Do any of the Backstreet Boys play an instrument?   **86**

[45] What was your relationship with the parents of the Backstreet Boys like?   **88**

[46] Did you ever hear Brian sing in church?   **90**

[47] Did any of the Backstreet Boys break their girlfriends' hearts?   **92**

[48] Why did you write this book?   **94**

[49] Did Brian go to college with you?   **96**

[50] How did your four-year relationship with Brian come to an end?   **100**

[1] How did you and Brian meet?

I knew Alex McLean (also known as A.J.), one of the Backstreet Boys, from the New Song Show Choir. New Song is a musical ensemble branching from the Osceola High School Chorus in Osceola, Florida. Alex was my partner in the show choir. Being a new member of New Song was hard on Alex, but we soon established a brother/sister relationship. We have always been really good friends and remain so today. One day, Alex came to class and told me he had joined a singing group put together by a local entrepreneur named Lou Pearlman. The freshly assembled group was the Backstreet Boys, and they sang at our chorus banquet. After the performance, Alex told me that one of the band members wanted my number. It was Brian. Alex said Brian was shy but really wanted to call me. Later I found out Alex was telling Brian the same thing, that I wanted his phone number! Alex was playing matchmaker the whole time. Of course, Brian and I had no idea. For some reason, Alex thought we would make a cute couple. I decided to give Alex my number so Brian could call me. That same night, Brian called. We stayed on the phone together for over three hours. We just immediately clicked. At that point, we simply had to see each other. We agreed to meet at a spot halfway between our homes.

You won't believe it, but the spot where we met was a Li'l Champ Convenience store off of John Young Highway in Kissimmee—not the most romantic place, to say the least! While I was waiting for him to show up, my car died.

No matter what I did, I just couldn't get it to start. I was so embarrassed when he showed up that I almost pretended it wasn't me he was supposed to meet. But when I saw him, I just had to get to know him better. He was so cute. We ended up having a good laugh about my car situation and eventually went back to my parents' place. We stayed up until three A.M., just talking. The attraction was so quick and mutual that we couldn't get enough of each other from that moment on.

> "The attraction was so quick and mutual that we couldn't get enough of each other from that moment on . . ."
>
> ♥

What were some romantic things Brian did for you?

In the beginning, we were both so taken by one another that we were constantly doing things for each other. One day while I was at school, Brian snuck into my locker and left dozens of roses, some frozen yogurt, and a note that said, "Meet me outside and we'll share." We both love frozen yogurt. That was very romantic, and I'll never forget it.

> "As tears flowed from his eyes, Brian said he loved me . . . "
>
> ♥

One of the most romantic things Brian ever did for me wasn't so private. A lot of the Backstreet Boys' songs are about our relationship. "That's What She Said" was written when we broke up for a brief period. The argument we got into hurt both of us. Brian put his feelings into words. Funny, our breakup lasted only two days, but the song will stand forever. Brian told me that he felt like the victim in our fight, and the song definitely reflects that. The song makes me out to be heartless, which isn't true. There are always two sides to an argument. I must not have been *too* heartless, because we did get back together. "That's What

She Said" still touches me when I hear it and really brings back some vivid memories. When we made up, he played the song for me, and the Boys recorded it soon after.

"Where Can We Go From Here" was written after our four-year relationship ended. Brian and I were best friends, and it's tough to let go of someone you're that close to. We were so young and needed to let each other go. We needed to grow, and we'd reached a point where it couldn't happen together anymore. Knowing all this didn't make anything easier, and the lyrics express the pain. Brian has mastered the art of putting his emotions into touching lyrics.

We also had a favorite song: "How Deep Is Your Love"—the Luther Vandross version. Brian even started performing it in concerts. Every time he did, I knew it was for me. I loved that.

Brian also gave me a "promise ring." The ring is a princess-cut diamond band he picked up in New York while the Boys were working in the recording studio. When he came home to Kissimmee, he led me up to my bedroom. As tears flowed from his eyes, Brian said he loved me and the ring was a promise that we would get married soon. He always thought we would get married and have a house full of kids. It was so cute. He even said that we'd have a son one day and name him Devon Thomas Littrell.

FUN FACTS!

Brian was known for singing on my answering machine and leaving roses in my locker at school. Pretty romantic!

[3] Do the Backstreet Boys wear boxers or briefs? Who looks the best in them?

FUN FACTS!

The Backstreet Boys wear both boxers and briefs—but Kevin looks the HOTTEST!

For the most part, the boys wear briefs. Brian wears both, but most often chooses briefs. Brian is very proud of his body (as he should be!) and loved to have pictures taken of himself in his underwear. He would pose for just about any picture.

> *"Kevin looks the best in his undergarments . . ."*
>
> ♥

Kevin looks the best in his undergarments. Kevin is very into his body and working out, so you'll often see him without a shirt. There is nothing hotter than Kevin pumping some iron! When I was on tour with the Boys, I enjoyed working out at the same time as Kevin. (Wouldn't you?)

I've been asked in the past why Nick never takes his shirt off like the rest of the band members. I think it's because he would rather impress people with his music than with his body. He's very proud of his music and his voice, and he should be. He's also a bit shy about his body, which I think is so cute.

[4] What do the Boys do before one of their concerts?

They usually do their own thing before the concert. The band gets along for the most part, which is cool. A lot of times they have competitions, like who can teach one of their guards to throw a football the farthest. In Europe they don't play American-style football, so it's a funny competition to watch.

> *"The boys are constantly playing pranks on each other . . . "*
>
> ♥

The boys are constantly playing pranks on each other. One night, Brian and Nick got together and after a little convincing by Brian, Nick pooped into a sock! Then they placed the sock inside the drummer's bass drum. That night during the show, every time their drummer, Tim, hit the bass drum, a terrible smell came out. Tim was so angry. He promised to get them back. Nick and Brian thought it was so funny that they barely made it through the concert.

But Tim did get back at Nick. The next night, he put melted chocolate all over the drumsticks and drums. When Nick went to play the drums, he got sticky chocolate all over him. Nick was professional about it, though. He finished the song and the show, covered with chocolate. We all had a good laugh about it that night.

[5] What was the prom like with Brian?

Brian and I were together for over four years, some of them during high school and some during my college years. We went to both my high-school prom and to college formals. The Backstreet Boys had such hectic schedules that Brian didn't know whether or not he would have time to go to the prom. Since Brian didn't attend my high school, I had to get a special permission slip signed so he would be allowed to go. Between his schedule and the permission slip I thought we would never make it to prom. To my delightful surprise, we did!

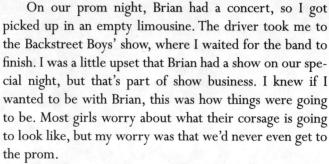

"On our prom night, Brian had a concert, so I got picked up in an empty limousine . . ."

On our prom night, Brian had a concert, so I got picked up in an empty limousine. The driver took me to the Backstreet Boys' show, where I waited for the band to finish. I was a little upset that Brian had a show on our special night, but that's part of show business. I knew if I wanted to be with Brian, this was how things were going to be. Most girls worry about what their corsage is going to look like, but my worry was that we'd never even get to the prom.

After he finished, we were both very excited to get to

the prom. When we did arrive, however, it was already pretty late. We got there just in time to take some pictures and mingle with a couple of my friends, but soon it was time to leave. Brian had arranged for us to stay at New Smyrna in a beautiful Victorian-style room on the beach. Kevin had told Brian about this spot. It was really special to Kevin because it was where he had told his girlfriend Kristen that he loved her. Brian and I were so tired from running from concert to prom that by the time we made it to the hotel we fell asleep almost immediately.

The next day we were rejuvenated and ready to see the town. There were lots of quaint stores surrounding the hotel. We spent the morning and most of the afternoon laughing and enjoying each other's company. Since there was no one around, Brian took our picture in the reflection of store windows. It was so funny. Brian had planned for Kevin to pick us up, because he knew the limo was dropping us off but not picking us up. In the late afternoon Kevin picked us up in the Bleeding Banana, as Brian's old Isuzu was called. It was a tight fit and very hot—the air conditioner wasn't working—but we made it home. Prom was great and New Smyrna was beautiful.

[6] Do any of the Backstreet Boys drink alcohol or take drugs?

For the most part, the band is very professional. Occasionally one of them will have too much to drink. I don't think any of the Backstreet Boys would ever advise taking drugs or drinking alcohol.

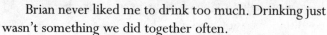

"One time Brian had too much to drink . . ."

Brian never liked me to drink too much. Drinking just wasn't something we did together often.

I do remember one time Brian had too much to drink. He called me from Europe and told me he wasn't feeling too good. He was actually pretty ill. I felt so bad for him. Brian drank too much because he was upset about a silly fight we had gotten into. We fought because we were frustrated about being apart from each other. Brian went to Alex's room to blow off some steam, and the two began to drink way too much. He was just experimenting, but consumed way too much alcohol in the process. Brian didn't know what his limits were and really paid the price for it. After getting really sick, he called to ask what to do to feel better. I told him to lie on his bed with one foot on the ground to keep the room from spinning. Brian swore never to drink again.

In all the time we spent together, Brian was never a regular or frequent heavy drinker. Even on his twenty-first birthday, he didn't go overboard. Alcohol is a substance that must be taken seriously and never abused. I know the Backstreet Boys don't think it's cool for girls to abuse alcohol, but they do know how to have a good time.

Howie did enjoy a good party, and there were times when he would get onto the tour bus a little hungover from a party the night before. One time in particular, the Backstreet Boys had to take a private jet to the city of their next show. I'll never forget the look on Howie's face as the plane began to take flight and experience a little turbulence. Being hungover and flying on a plane isn't a good combo. Let's just say that Howie chilled from the parties for a few extra days.

[7] Do any of the Backstreet Boys have girlfriends?

This is a question I get a lot. It's a very difficult question to answer, because you never know when a relationship will end or begin. I have watched dozens of different girls come and go for each of the band members. They've had a lot of girlfriends. At one time or another, all of the boys had girlfriends while I was with Brian.

"Howie was always so romantic . . ."

The girlfriends I spent the most time with were Kristen, Sabina, and Marissa. Kristen dated Kevin for years. She was always a beautiful girl inside and out. Kristen looks like a model—she was actually a Rockette. Kristen has the prettiest cheekbones, beautiful dark blond hair, and a dancer's body, to top it off. Sabina dated Howie for a while and was around a lot when the Backstreet Boys had their tours in Europe. Howie was always so romantic with her. He liked to love on Sabina whenever possible. Sabina has big beautiful brown eyes and can dance anyone under the table. Marissa was Alex's girl, and they were always interesting to watch. The two of them had energy to spare. Marissa looks a lot like her mother who was part of Wright Stuff management, which was the Backstreet Boys original management. Only one of the boys never had a longtime girlfriend while Brian and I were seeing each other. Nick was never one to be tied down. He was too busy flirting with all the girls and playing Nintendo.

Of course, since they are so popular, they are going to have girlfriends. Look at it this way: since you know that they've had girlfriends in the past, then you know that you could be the next one. Which Backstreet Boy would you want to call your boyfriend? All the Backstreet Boys' girlfriends, including me, were very normal. They never seemed to go for really flashy girls. If it could happen to us, it could happen to you. A future band member might be right under your nose now. That shy boy you sit next to in chorus class could be the next Alex!

[8] What do Brian and the Backstreet Boys enjoy doing when they aren't performing? What do they do in their spare time?

Brian and the boys have a lot of hobbies. They like sports, video games, and girls. Brian lived at my parents' house, a.k.a. the Stonebraker Pad (that's how he referred to it in the thank-you of his albums) for over two years. He became very close with my family, especially my little brothers, Steven and John. Steven and Brian are the closest in age and have a lot of the same hobbies. They both love basketball. Brian really admired my brother's skills, and they played together all the time. In the video for "We've Got It Goin' On," there is a scene of Nick and Brian playing basketball with my brother Steven. The director wanted to show the ball going through the hoop. Nick and Brian were so nervous, because it was their first video shoot, they couldn't make a basket. The director ended up taking shots of Brian and Nick shooting and then brought my brother in to actually make the shots!

Brian and Steven spent a lot of their free time together and grew very close. Brian even sang the national anthem at Steven's high-school basketball games. Brian liked to spend time with the rest of my family as well. He would umpire my little brother John's Little League games and reminisce about his own playing days. One of Brian's most embarrassing moments occurred while he was playing Little League. He got so nervous that he had an "accident." He also enjoyed braiding my sister Mari's hair while he sang "The Most Beautiful Girl in the World."

Brian and the other Boys love to sleep in. The band's beauty sleep is very important to them. I know this sounds like a weird hobby, but when you have a schedule like the Backstreet Boys, sleeping in is a luxury. I remember days when I hardly saw Brian until one in the afternoon. When Brian had a lazy day, he would lounge on the couch and watch talk shows all day.

The boys also love to play golf. Brian is ambidextrous but does most things right-handed except play golf. Brian and Nick even played in their spare time at a photo shoot in Hawaii. I'm telling you, every chance they got, they were out on the golf course.

"The band's beauty sleep is very important . . ."

♥

FUN FACTS!

During their spare time on tour, the Backstreet Boys enjoy to riding go-carts and playing video games.

[9] Were you ever with Brian when he encountered his biggest fear?

Of course I know you fans are hip to all Backstreet trivia, and know that Brian's biggest fear is heights. He avoids doing almost everything where heights are involved. However, there are times when he just can't avoid doing some things. In fact, the most memorable story I have about Brian and his fear took place in the mountains, during the filming of the European version of "I'll Never Break Your Heart." The Backstreet Boys had to take a trolley up to the top of a mountain in Utah where the video was filmed. The idea was to film the boys coming down the mountain with some female models. That's a fine idea, but the trick was how to get Brian to the top. He was absolutely against the idea of going up, but with some coaching from the band and myself, we got him on the trolley. I had to ride with him to console him because he was so nervous. We ended up lying at the base of the lift so Brian wouldn't notice how high we were going. When you confront your biggest fear, it can be horrifying. Brian became faint and his breathing shallow. To get his mind off the mountain, I told him to picture himself playing basketball with Steven.

Meanwhile, Nick and the other boys were talking about what a scene it was and how everything was so beautiful. Of course they were right, but they weren't helping me trick Brian. After many nerve-racking minutes, we all finally made it to the top of the mountain. I was so proud of Brian! Brian later told me that coming down was no big deal because his mind was on filming and being professional.

Brian also hates roller coasters with a passion. On his twenty-first birthday, he and I went to Disney World. We went on Thunder Mountain, which at the time was Disney's scariest roller coaster ride. I think Brian was afraid of the roller coaster because it looks so scary when you're watching other people ride it. It took some convincing, but I finally got Brian to give it a shot. He was confronting his fear head-on. And once I got him on the roller coaster, I couldn't get him off. He loved it, and I was so proud of him for facing one of his biggest fears.

What is your biggest fear? Follow Brian's lead and confront it—but be safe.

> "Brian became faint and his breathing shallow . . ."
>
> ♥

[10] How have the Backstreet Boys changed because of their success?

> "Fame and money have had their effects on the band . . . "
>
> ♥

Success has definitely changed the Backstreet Boys. I remember what they were all like when the band first started. They've matured a lot since then. But fame and money have had their effects on the band. One of the best examples is their obsession with cars. In the beginning, most of the boys drove very old used cars. Brian's car was by far the funniest. It was a red Isuzu low-rider truck with yellow splashes of paint. We called it the Bleeding Banana. I never quite understood why Brian loved that car so much. He ended up getting rid of it after someone went to the bathroom in the front seat (my ex-boyfriend), a very cruel joke. From there, Brian moved onto a Honda Civic. This is when his tire fetish began. He just loved tires and wheels. He ended up replacing the Honda's wheels, though there was no need. By this time, Brian and the rest of the Boys had come into some money through the royalties from their record sales. That's when all the Boys started to get a little crazy. Howie was very conservative at first—he was very carefully with his money. Eventually, however, even he broke down and bought a house and a Corvette. It was soon pretty common for all the boys to buy Mercedeses and BMWs. Now, they have several cars and trucks each. The spending didn't stop with cars, either. It expanded to clothes, jewelry, and even houses. Alex is known for his jewelry fetish. It is not uncommon for Alex to go into a jewelry store and spend thousands of dollars at one time! Some of the Backstreet Boys have houses in a couple of cities. Now that's big time.

As for their personalities changing, I have to say that they all have stayed sweet. They care about their fans and love what they do.

FUN FACTS!

When the Backstreet Boys weren't famous, Brian would love to drive my grandmother's convertible Mercedes and dream of the days when he could afford to buy one.

What was the funniest moment you shared with the Backstreet Boys?

FUN FACTS!

Brian's first car was a low-rider truck we called the Bleeding Banana because of the color—red with yellow splashes. The Bleeding Banana broke down one night while Brian and I were in the car driving on a major highway. It was almost eleven and we had to walk to a phone to call my dad to pick us up. In short, the Backstreet Boys didn't always have limos chauffeuring them around!

I experienced some hilarious times with the Boys. I actually caught one of the funniest ones on camera. They were in the middle of a photo shoot that was becoming a little boring. I got them to play around a bit, and we came up with the idea of shooting them in the bathroom. The band stood there pretending to use the facilities and all looked back at me for the shot. It was really pretty funny and livened up the day's shoot. They will pose for just about any picture for a good laugh. The Backstreet Boys are known for joking around, and everything is usually done in good fun. Feeling at home and just being themselves is when the Backstreet Boys are at the top of their game. The Boys pose for so many photos that it can become boring after a while, so they try to mix it up as frequently as possible.

> *"We came up with the idea of shooting them in the bathroom . . ."*
>
> ♥

For instance, the Boys had a blast filming the last scene of the European version of the video for "I'll Never Break Your Heart." The scene was a big snowball fight. Playing in the snow allowed the Boys to simply be boys for a change. Brian's favorite part of the video is when he throws a snowball at Nick and hits him right on the head. When you watch the video you can tell it's a moment of real, actual joy for both of them. Look for this interaction between Brian and Nick the next time you watch the video.

[12]

How do Brian and his loved ones cope with his heart condition?

I'm sure everyone is aware, to some extent, of Brian's terrible heart problems. Living through this was and is a struggle for Brian. Brian has always known about his condition, a heart murmur at birth that was later complicated by a staph infection. Brian and his family had assumed his heart was getting stronger until one fateful day in Orlando, Florida.

> *"The doctor's appointment lasted just minutes but shook Brian to tears . . . ."*

Brian's parents knew he had an appointment with a highly regarded doctor, so they flew down from Kentucky to be with him. The incomplete closure in Brian's heart was supposed to have corrected itself as Brian aged, but out of the blue we found out differently. The doctor's appointment lasted just minutes but shook Brian to tears. His family and I were by his side to comfort him. What do you say or do when you want so desperately to help someone? I wanted so much just to trade places with him, to take his pain away. All I could offer was a shoulder to cry on and my prayers.

After the appointment, Brian and I drove away in our car and his parents in theirs. As they pulled away, I could see his mom break down into tears. She had stayed strong in front of Brian, but let it all out as soon as she was away from him. Brian's mom had lived with this fear for Brian's entire life; the possibility of heart surgery was closer than ever.

Brian lived with the idea of surgery in the back of his mind for over a year before he endured it. By the time of the actual surgery, we had broken up. I only found out that it was coming up because Brian told my mom. Even though Brian and I were no longer boyfriend and girlfriend, we had been best friends for four years; I was so sad. I called Brian immediately to tell him my prayers were with him for the operation.

I didn't see Brian again until shortly after the operation. We had bought a Jeep together, and met to sign off on the loan papers. My brother Steven came with me because they were still close friends. Brian looked a little rundown, but seemed in good spirits as he showed my brother his scar. I'm told through mutual friends that Brian's health has never been better. The power of prayer should never be underestimated.

[13] What are Brian's favorite foods? What are the special recipes that he likes most?

Like the old saying goes, the way to a man's heart is through his stomach. Brian is no exception. He may not look it, but Brian loves food and likes it to be prepared "Brian style." Brian absolutely adores Pillsbury Cinnamon Rolls, but only the small size. He won't even touch the jumbos. The secret to making these rolls perfect for B-Rok is the icing. After the rolls are fresh out of the oven, steaming hot, the icing must be placed only in the center, allowing it to melt over the sides of the bun. This is serious business, and Brian is strict about this procedure.

> *"In case you're wondering, Brian does drink the milk at the bottom of the bowl . . ."*
>
> ♥

One of Brian's favorite homemade dishes is mac'n' cheese. Once again, there is a trick to making it for Brian. There must be a perfect combination of macaroni and cheese, there has to be a slight amount more of cheese than macaroni. Most importantly, the dish must be topped with Ritz crackers. Don't try to substitute a different brand of cracker, because Brian will know the difference. Another homemade meal Brian liked to dig into was my mom's meat loaf. Brian couldn't get enough of my mom's cooking when he lived with us. Brian would come home from rehearsals and go straight to my mom for food, food, and food. Although cereal isn't homemade, Brian still loves it. At the Stonebraker pad, there is always a cabinet full of cereal, a favorite snack between meals. Brian was never picky with brands of cereal; but the sweeter, the better. Fruity Pebbles, Life, and Corn Pops were some of his favorites. (In case you're wondering, Brian does drink the milk at the bottom of the bowl.)

When you're on the go as much as Brian is, fast food is sometimes the only option. All the Backstreet Boys love McDonald's. I can't count how many times we went there while touring! When Brian is in Kissimmee, Florida, he always goes to DeAngelos to get a steak n' cheese. He would usually pick up more than one at a time; he just couldn't get enough. When Brian had more time, he liked to go to Red Lobster and chow down on the Caesar salad with chicken. Yummy.

If you really want to get on Brian's (or most guys') good side, try candy. Pez candy is the best—Brian loves all the different character dispensers.

So now you know the secrets to keeping B-Rok fed and happy, just in case you ever have Brian as a houseguest.

[14] Were you ever around when the Backstreet Boys filmed their videos? What were they like?

> "Remember the scene in the "We've Got It Goin' On" video with Nick and Brian washing a Jeep?"
>
> ♥

During the four years I dated Brian, I was present at almost all the photo and video shoots. I wanted to be there to give the boys my support. I even appeared in the Backstreet Boys' first video, "We've Got It Goin' On." Since this was the first video, the budget was very low—no glitz and glamour, just a lot of fun. Not only did I appear in this video, but my brother Steven, other Boys' girlfriends, friends, and even my car got to make cameo appearances. Remember the scene with Nick and Brian washing a Jeep? That was my Jeep, and I was the girl washing it with them. I must admit that even though this was a video, the situation was not farfetched. The boys always wanted to play ball. My favorite part of the video is when I act like I'm going to kiss Brian and instead squirt him with water. Brian and I laughed so hard filming that part of the video. Everything was filmed in a day, but what an experience! Behind the scenes, the filming of "We've Got It Goin' On" was low-key and a family affair.

Another video I enjoyed being present for was the filming of "Quit Playing Games With My Heart." The filming took only one day, but what a long day it was. The filming had to be mastered in a day because the Backstreet Boys were scheduled to fly to Southeast Asia the day after. "Quit Playing Games With My Heart" was filmed at Howard Middle School in Orlando, Florida. Looking at the finished product the video looks fairly simple, but it was the schedule that added such stress. Brian, for example, had two hours after the filming was completed to arrive at an appointment at the hospital to get the recommended standard shots for traveling to Southeast Asia. After Brian's appointment he had less than two hours to be at the airport ready to fly to Southeast Asia with the Backstreet Boys. Wow, what a schedule, but it paid off because "Quit Playing Games With My Heart" is one hot video!

FUN FACTS!

"Quit Playing Games With My Heart" was filmed at a local middle school in Orlando called Howard Middle. The filming lasted throughout the night and the film crew had to bring in sprinklers for the rain scenes. The Backstreet Boys were drenched—but sexier than ever!

[15] Do the Backstreet Boys ever wear makeup?

Of course they do! How else do you think the Backstreet Boys have those year-round perfect complexions? During shows, video and photo shoots, the Backstreet Boys must look their best. They are normal people just like you and me and sometimes need makeup to cover up imperfections. I'm sure you've noticed Brian's eyes being bluer than normal in certain videos. Sometimes he wears colored contacts, and often the photographers even use trick photography to make these cuties look even hotter. When I was on tour with the Backstreet Boys, Brian would wake up early every morning to use self-tanners. He knew the sun was bad for him but still wanted that golden glow. There were a few times when Brian got carried away with the self-tanner. Brian would not only be tinted orange but have streaks on the palm of his hands. I'm sure if you have ever tried this option to tanning, you've had this happen to you.

> *"There were a few times that Brian got carried away with the self-tanner . . . "*
>
> ♥

Back in the very beginning of the Backstreet Boys' career, they would do just about anything as long as the video camera was rolling or photos were being taken. They had stars in their eyes and dreamed of having the popularity they hold today. For a good laugh, Nick and Brian dressed up as girls. They went the whole nine yards—wigs, dresses, and tacky makeup. It was hilarious. Nick and Brian really got into it. But make no mistake: Nick and Brian aren't gay (although there is nothing wrong with being gay). The Boys were simply joking around. Singing and walking, they did everything like a girl would. I must add that they were very pretty girls, go girl Backstreet power.

[16]   Is Brian a good kisser?

This is one of the questions I'm most often asked. The answer is yes—he's a great kisser! It's nice to have the same style of kissing with your boyfriend. Kissing is a sweet way to show your affection for someone. The Backstreet Boys' management didn't like them to show any public display of affection. They felt that the fans wouldn't like it. This made things hard; imagine not being able to give your boyfriend a sweet kiss when you wanted. All we heard was "No PDAs!"—public displays of affection. When I think back, it was kind of funny.

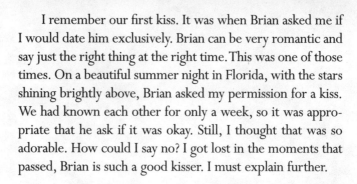

"I remember our first kiss . . . "

I remember our first kiss. It was when Brian asked me if I would date him exclusively. Brian can be very romantic and say just the right thing at the right time. This was one of those times. On a beautiful summer night in Florida, with the stars shining brightly above, Brian asked my permission for a kiss. We had known each other for only a week, so it was appropriate that he ask if it was okay. Still, I thought that was so adorable. How could I say no? I got lost in the moments that passed, Brian is such a good kisser. I must explain further.

Brian has small measurements so his kisses are perfect for a girl's small mouth. I've never received a sloppy kiss from Brian. I don't think there is anything worse than a real live spit-bath from your boyfriend, yuck! Brian knows how to change the emotion of his kiss to the mood of the moment, very important.

Brian and I were always kissing and happened to kiss one too many times around my little sister Mari. Mari was very young at the time so she started tattling on me to our mother for kissing. She ran to my mom and said, "Brian and Samantha are 'mooching.' " We got the biggest laugh out of her saying mooching instead of smooching. From that moment on, "mooch" was a favorite word between Brian and me. We would be anywhere, in front of anybody and ask each other for a "mooch." No one ever knew what in the world we were talking about, it was great.

[17]

Were there ever any hard times with the Backstreet Boys?

Fame and money sometimes invite new problems. As settings change in your life, sometimes your relationships must change as well. Though the Backstreet Boys love what they do, there are sacrifices that must be made. For instance, Nick, being the youngest member, had a hard time with the demanding schedule. Sometimes he would cry because he missed his family and needed some free time. I remember one meeting at the Backstreet Boys' office in particular. The Boys had been going nonstop but had to meet to go over their new schedules. When Nick discovered that he didn't have any time off, he almost had a breakdown. Nick was not being spoiled. During the early days, their management didn't give the Boys time to even breathe. Once, I was backstage with the band before a European concert. Nick was so sick. The show was about to begin, and he was vomiting backstage. The show had to go on, so Nick did perform. He was so sick throughout the concert. Every break Nick got he was backstage getting sick. He would then go back up onstage with a big smile on his face and act like nothing was wrong. The tour manager did nothing to help Nick; he was expected to perform. Fortunately, the Backstreet Boys do not have this management group any longer.

Brian had his share of stress too. One time, Brian had to

learn and record two of the Backstreet Boys' hits in just two days. Since he had the lead in both songs, the pressure was overwhelming, and as a result he developed fever blisters—not only on his lips, but also on his face, under his eye and on his cheek. He said it hurt so bad to have makeup applied for an appearance.

> "Every break Nick got he was backstage getting sick . . . "
>
> ♥

The tension on tour is also enormous and eventually catches up with everyone. It hit Alex hard in Europe. At one point Alex had to have his stomach pumped: the combination of stress and drinking too much orange juice eventually got to him. The doctor ordered Alex to lay off any acidic drinks. Like Nick, Alex still performed through his illness.

Sometimes being the hottest band around can have its disadvantages, but for the most part the Boys enjoy what they do. What really keeps the Backstreet Boys going strong through all the pressure and stress is their fans. The fans are the real inspiration for all the Boys.

What was it like being a girlfriend of one of the Backstreet Boys? How did you get along with the other members?

Dating a member of one of the most popular bands in the world can be fun and exciting, but at the same time it's difficult. During much of my relationship with Brian, the Backstreet Boys were very well known in Europe but not in the United States. This situation was a little funny, because the Boys would get mobbed getting on a plane in Europe, but not a soul would be around when the plane landed in the States. Getting along with the Backstreet Boys was the easiest part of dating Brian. They are pretty cool guys. My relationship was stronger with some of the Boys. Alex and I were always tight because we knew each other the longest. We liked to reminisce about being partners in our show choir in high school. Sometimes we would break into song and dance, the other Boys would just laugh at us. I was closest with Nick, probably because Brian cared so much about him. Another bond I had with Nick is his age, he is around the same age as my brother Steven. Whenever I was around Nick I felt like I had my little brother with me. My relationship with Howie and Kevin was about the same. I got along with both very well. They were older and more mature, I identified with them even though I was younger.

The hardest part about dating Brian was the secrecy to

the public. Management knew they couldn't keep the Boys from dating but stressed that the public shouldn't know it. When I was on tour with the Backstreet Boys, I loved meeting the fans and enjoyed watching them react to their idols. I wanted the fans to be able to meet the Boys. I would take pictures for fans whenever possible. The problem was that the fans didn't know who I was and often became suspicious and angry because fans thought I was trying to take the Backstreet Boys away from them.

> "The hardest part about dating Brian was the secrecy . . ."
>
> ♥

The confusion about who the girlfriends were led to some horrible memories of traveling with the Backstreet Boys. One memory really sticks out in my mind. When we were on tour, it was standard for the Boys to walk in front of the girlfriends. The Boys would load their tour bus first, with their bodyguards leading the way. The girlfriends would be left to fend for themselves. This particular day, the fans were exceptionally anxious because they had been waiting outside the hotel for the Boys all night. As I ran down the roped-off area from the hotel to the tour bus, the crowd blocked my entrance to the bus—not intentionally, but the fans wanted one last look at the Backstreet Boys. This left me in a scary situation. I was in the middle of a mob with no way out. Everyone was pushing, trying for a glimpse of the band. I was scared that I'd get trampled by the mob and left behind as the bus pulled away. Luckily, security came to my rescue, but it was a scary experience.

Was Brian really bitten by a spider?

Not only is it true, but I was by Brian's side through the whole ordeal. I'll never forget Brian coming to me one morning and saying, "I think I have a boil." A boil is an infection on the skin, which is exactly what the bite looked like. Brian had shown the area of his leg to Kevin, who was living with him at the time. Kevin quickly told him to get boil medication to draw out the infection. For over a week Brian religiously applied his medication, until he noticed that it was getting worse, not better. This alarmed all of us. Brian was in rehearsal all hours of the day and wasn't able to dance because of the pain. Finally, he broke down and reluctantly went to his doctor, who told Brian that he had been bitten by a spider—and not just any spider but a brown recluse, one of the deadliest spiders known to man. Brian's face showed his pain as the doctor began cutting the infected area from his leg. If any of the poison had been left in Brian's leg, it would have eaten away at the muscle. Brian left the doctor's office on crutches but thankful that the infected bite had been caught in time.

> "Brian religiously applied his medication until he noticed that it was getting worse, not better . . . "

Brian will always have a scar on his leg as a reminder of the close encounter he had with the spider. We never could figure out how or where he got bit. We thought that maybe it happened at the warehouse where the Backstreet Boys were rehearsing. We'll never know for sure, but what a scary experience! Brian never could get over the idea that a small spider placed him on crutches for weeks.

What is Brian most sensitive about?

Brian is really sensitive about his height and weight. He always has been and probably always will be overly concerned about it. He would try to make his foot size bigger by wearing double socks. It actually worked. Brian would tell me childhood stories of being compared to his cousin, fellow band member Kevin. A comparison of family members isn't unusual, especially with two boys around the same age. The problem was that Kevin had a bigger frame than Brian. Kevin was always such a strong, muscular boy, and Brian simply couldn't keep up. Brian's mom would reminisce about Brian as a young boy, of how she would take him and his older brother to Burger King to split a Whopper Jr. between the three of them. Brian was never a big eater growing up. He told me about being the smallest baseball player on his team, and ordering extra-small pants. Brian could never make a playing position on his high-school basketball team. Not to fret—he was recognized as a key player on his church basketball team. Good thing, because that's where he learned to sing. Although a head or two shorter than the rest of the players on the basketball court, according to my brother Steven, Brian has a great outside shot. Why worry about dunking for only two points when you can make three from the outside? Steven says that Brian's heart was always in the game and that's what made up for his size.

Girls, remember, tell Brian his size is perfect, because he's sensitive about it and needs encouragement.

Remind him that good things sometimes do come in a small package.

> "Good things sometimes do come in a
> small package . . ."
>
> ♥

[21] What was it like going home with Brian to Kentucky?

The first time I was invited to go home with Brian to Kentucky, I wasn't allowed to go. I was in high school, and my parents didn't think I needed to miss school to go to Kentucky. Since I couldn't go to Kentucky, Brian's parents came to Florida to meet me. We had heard so much about each other, it was like we were old friends. When Brian's parents walked off the plane, I knew immediately who they were without an introduction. Brian is a perfect combination of both. Brian always said that he got his dad's thin hair and his mom's sensitive side. If you've ever wondered what Brian will look like later in life, look to his father for the answer. Brian looks just like his father did when he was younger. Like father, like son.

> "He wanted people to like him for who he truly was, not just because he was a Backstreet Boy . . ."
>
> ♥

Brian and I graduated from high school the same year, just weeks apart. After moving to Orlando because of the Backstreet Boys, Brian enrolled in correspondence courses in Florida. This allowed him to stay on the same page as his high-school class in Kentucky. When it was time to graduate, Brian had no problem going back to Kentucky to walk

40

with his class. Just weeks before Brian's graduation, I received my diploma from Osceola High School. Brian was present for my graduation and even sang with my chorus class during the ceremony. Since I was a graduate, my parents couldn't use school as an excuse and gave me permission to go to Brian's graduation at Tate's Creek High School in Kentucky. Brian and I were so excited; I got to meet all his extended family and friends. Upon Brian's return to Tate's Creek High School, he noticed a difference in the way he was treated by his classmates. Once a social average joe, he was now the hippest guy at school. Brian wasn't comfortable with this. He wanted people to like him for who he truly was, not just because he was a Backstreet Boy.

During Brian's graduation ceremony, he wore my tassel on top of his. He was full of smiles and thrilled to have his family present. I was particularly fond of Brian's father's parents. They were extremely sweet and full of life. Brian's grandmother gave me a pair of her earrings for Christmas one year. The earrings are large gold loops, absolutely precious. The sentimental value of that kind of gift is immeasurable. There was one family member missing though: Kevin. Kevin was in New York with his girlfriend Kristen. Because of the hectic Backstreet Boys schedule, Brian's graduation was the only time off for all of the Boys. This put Kevin in a difficult situation, but he decided to go visit Kristen instead of being present at Brian's graduation. Brian was hurt by his absence.

He was so hurt because Brian remembered being present at Kevin's graduation. Brian recalled having severe sunburn and experiencing a lot of discomfort, but still sitting through the entire ceremony to see his cousin graduate. Brian didn't understand why Kevin couldn't make a sacrifice for him. Brian's graduation from Tate's Creek High School was a success and lots of fun. High-school graduation is so important. It only happens once, and I'm so happy that I was there for Brian, and he for me.

[22]

Did you go to the same high school as any of the Backstreet Boys?

I went to high school with Alex. We were singing partners in the New Song Show Choir at Osceola High School in Kissimmee, Florida. Alex was two grades below me: I was a junior and he was a freshman. I wasn't sure what to think of this freshman named Alex who was my new New Song partner—he was young, and I'd never heard him sing before. But Alex and I soon bonded and became great partners. At times while Alex was singing baritone, he would get off-key, go extremely flat, but he always tried. We had an awesome choral instructor, Mr. Carswell. He could get anyone to sing on-key. When it came to dancing, Alex was the best. He caught on quickly to the choreography and looked sharp. For one of our chorus fundraisers, Alex sang "Johnny B. Goode." He brought the house down. Everyone was shocked to see that he had such a dynamic stage presence, because he had never shown it in class.

> *"I wasn't sure what to think of this fresh-
> man named Alex . . . "*
>
> ♥

    I wasn't surprised when Alex came to class soon after and told me that he had been chosen in an audition to be a member of a new group being created by a businessman in Orlando. I must admit that I was one of the few who believed in him. A lot of the kids at school felt the Backstreet Boys were not going to make it to the big time. Alex sure proved them wrong! Alex soon dropped out of school and enrolled in correspondence courses along with Brian and Nick. They had such demanding schedules that they couldn't go to normal classes. I bet you wish you could have been a student in that classroom!

Alex came back to Osceola High School at the end of the year for the chorus banquet. The newly formed Backstreet Boys performed at the banquet. This is when Alex introduced me to Brian. Everyone at the chorus banquet loved the Backstreet Boys' first performance. The girls fell in love with the cute boys immediately. This took place in 1993—not that long ago, when you think about it. With a little time and a lot of hard work, the Backstreet Boys have made it to the big leagues. They really proved that you should never forget your dreams, because they really can come true.

FUN FACTS!

I was Alex's singing partner in a show choir in high school. Alex wasn't always an outgoing Backstreet Boy; in high school he was shy—and tattoo-less.

What was the best trip you took with the Backstreet Boys?

The best trip I took with the Backstreet Boys was to a photo shoot in Hawaii. The boys were there for business, so I tagged along for fun. The photo shoot was for a European magazine willing to take the Boys to the most beautiful spots on the island just to get the perfect shot. I, of course, *had* to tag along. This was a once-in-a-lifetime chance to see Hawaii. I could try to explain the beauty of the scenery, but I wouldn't do it justice.

> *"I think Alex mainly wanted to be on the beach to flirt with girls . . . "*
>
> ♥

When the Backstreet Boys weren't working in Hawaii, they were having fun. We would play all sorts of sports, depending on who was there and the mood we were in. The Hawaiian favorite was tennis. We played it almost non-stop. Not all the boys participated, but we got quite a game going. The teams were Nick and Brian against Nick's mom, Jane Carter, and me. Nick's little brother, Aaron, acted as our ball boy. Poor little guy—our lack of skill gave him a tremendous workout! The tennis courts were right on the ocean and the view was breathtaking. We could look to one side and see the ocean and to the other to see the rain forest. Jane and Brian are good tennis players, so Nick and I acted as team buffers, equaling out the competition. It was the boys vs. the girls, and the stakes were high. The pressure was on. Nick and Brian will want to get me for boasting about this, but the girls won several more time than the boys did. I don't know if it was girl power or Jane's skills, or maybe a combination of both. Jane and I made a great team. She's such a hip mom. Of course, Nick sure didn't think so, as he was losing to his mom!

When we weren't playing tennis, we were body-surfing. The waves in Hawaii are the real deal and are so much fun. Alex joined the body-surfing activities. I think Alex mainly wanted to be on the beach to flirt with girls. Regardless, we had a party going on, especially at night when a few of us would get together for dinner. Hawaii has the most delicious seafood.

There was one thing Brian forgot to do while in the middle of this paradise . . . his laundry. Immediately following the Hawaiian photo shoot, the Boys had to take a trip to Los Angeles to prepare for the filming of "Backstreet's Back." Brian spent his last evening in Hawaii—where else but in the Laundromat!

FUN FACTS!

For good luck before a flight, Brian would place his right hand on the plane and tell the "big bird" to take us home safely.

[24] How do the Backstreet Boys get along?

All of the Backstreet Boys get along for the most part. Some of the members are closer than others. It's hard to be surrounded by the same people day in and day out for so long and not fight once in a while. Imagine getting four of your friends and spending every second together. Do you think you would ever fight? Probably—but you would have a good time too, wouldn't you?

> *"Kevin was involved in most of the fights. Howie in the least . . ."*

Kevin was involved in most of the fights; Howie in the least. As a matter of fact, Howie was never in any argument that I saw. Howie is by far the mellowest of the group and tries to mind his own business. Brian and Kevin have had some heated arguments. They really know how to push each other's buttons. Maybe it's because they are cousins, I don't know, but it can get ugly. Kevin and Brian would fight mostly about their attitudes clashing. They are very different people with different personalities; they don't always understand each other. Kevin is stronger, but Brian has the worse temper. One time the two got into such a fight that the limo driver had to stop the car and pull to the side of the road. The driver told them that he wouldn't drive until they calmed down. But don't worry, I've seen Brian and Kevin hug a lot more than I've seen them fight. None of the other Backstreet Boys would fight over anything specific. Fights were usually started because the Boys needed space from each other. Living on top of someone can instigate fights. Name-calling usually fueled theses types of arguments.

Nick and Brian were very close and loved each other like brothers. They seem to really understand and respect each other. I think it helps that they have some of the same hobbies, because it allows them to spend a lot of their free time together. They both are family oriented. The Backstreet Boys will probably always remain friends.

[25] Tell us a good story about the Backstreet Boys before they were famous.

FUN FACTS!

Did you know that whenever Brian would meet a child he loved to speak in his Donald Duck voice?

Everyone knows who the Backstreet Boys are now, but there was a time when no one knew of this hot group, especially in the United States. The best story I have occurred about four years ago. The Boys were popular in Europe but nobodies in the States. They were always trying to catch their big break and become known at home, but it took a while before this dream became a reality. To promote themselves, the Backstreet Boys would make appearances at different radio stations around the United States. At these promotions the stations would hold contests where the listeners could call in to win different prizes. One prize was a dinner with the Boys, a type of meet-and-greet for the winner. The listeners called in, and a lucky few won. But when the Boys arrived to the dinner to meet the winners, they had a rude awakening: the contest winners didn't have a clue who the Backstreet Boys were. They were under the impression that they were to have dinner with Blackstreet, a popular group at the time. The Backstreet Boys were so embarrassed, but they understood the mistake, because the group names do sound alike. The Boys didn't stay for dinner but got a good laugh out of the evening. Now, in 1999, only four years later, there is no way a mistake like that could occur!

"The contest winners did not have a clue who the Backstreet Boys were . . . "

♥

49

[26] What were the parties like at Lou Pearlman's house?

If ever a party needed to be had, Lou Pearlman was always ready to throw it. Lou is the creator of the Backstreet Boys and assisted in the success of many other groups. 'N Sync is one of the other big ones. I'm sure you can imagine how much fun these parties could be. There were people there from all walks of life, and it was a guarantee you would meet someone interesting. The parties would go on forever, with wonderful food, music, and plenty of dancing. Alex was always the first to show off his moves. Howie and Kevin were the two most likely to stay for the entire party. They were real night owls. Nick would sometimes be in Tampa and not have the energy to come; a Backstreet Boys schedule will do that to you. Brian was more of a homebody and didn't like to stay out late. He enjoyed more intimate settings with one-on-one conversation instead of a big party.

> *"Brian enjoyed more intimate settings . . . "*
>
>

I'll never forget Brian being challenged to sing at one of Lou's parties. There was a young guy there who wanted to show his talent. There were always people trying to capture the spotlight in an effort to get their big break. This guy put Brian on the spot—kind of like a sing-off to find out who was better. This was not Brian's style, but he wasn't about to back down. A section of the room got quiet while the singing began. The guy who challenged Brian began to belt out a gospel song as loud as he could to gain attention. Brian politely let him finish then began to sing "One Last Cry," one of his favorite Brian McKnight's songs. Brian didn't need to use volume to impress, he simply caresses each note and pleased the crowd. It was no surprise when Brian showed this guy up. Brian's voice is amazing. It's hard to beat that type of talent.

[27] Did Brian ever do anything to make you mad?

One major argument comes to mind. It was my brother Steven's eighteenth birthday, and Brian thought it would be hilarious to surprise him at my parents' house. Well, I thought a surprise party sounded like a great idea at the time, but little did I know what Brian was up to. I should have known something was up when Brian asked my parents to leave the house for the evening. When he started calling all of Steven's friends, I began to get a little nervous.

> "I thought the party sounded like a great idea at the time, but little did I know what Brian was up to."
>
> ♥

It wasn't until the "show" started that I knew what was really happening. But by that time, it was already too late. Brian's great idea was to celebrate Steven's birthday by having two female dancers perform for Steven and his friends. I thought this was a terrible idea, and I let Brian know it. I stormed out of the room, yelling at him in my loudest voice. In my mind, he was corrupting my little brother—something I wouldn't allow. But ultimately Brian won out. And honestly, I'd thought it was going to be a lot worse than it was. The two girls ended up just dancing and teasing the boys a bit. The whole thing had turned into a huge argument that got way out of hand. I may have gone a bit overboard, but I really did feel he was out of line. Brian later apologized, saying it was only done in good fun. We made up and everything was fine. For the record, Steven wants me to say that it was the best party he has ever had. The guys loved it—go figure.

[28] What was a typical date like with Brian? Did you ever double-date with other members of the Backstreet Boys?

Brian didn't like to go out very often. He definitely preferred hanging out at home to a night on the town. But once in a while we would go out, and he'd take me to meet up with some friends at a local hangout. If we went out for dinner, the most likely place we would end up was Red Lobster. Brian isn't a big fan of seafood but loves their Caesar salad.

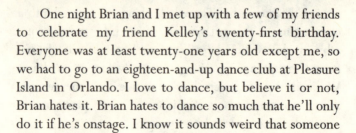

"The night ended with the girls dancing and the boys flirting . . ."

One night Brian and I met up with a few of my friends to celebrate my friend Kelley's twenty-first birthday. Everyone was at least twenty-one years old except me, so we had to go to an eighteen-and-up dance club at Pleasure Island in Orlando. I love to dance, but believe it or not, Brian hates it. Brian hates to dance so much that he'll only do it if he's onstage. I know it sounds weird that someone who dances so well onstage and in the boys' videos wouldn't like to dance for fun, but it's true. Brian's weird about having to have every dance move choreographed like it is during their concerts. So we compromised: Brian and most of his friends sat on the couches in the corner while my friends and I hit the dance floor. And while we girls were dancing, Brian and the boys ran into some European Backstreet Boys fans. Brian was so proud, because this was before the band was really popular in the United States. He got to show his American friends that he actually was popular and well known, but only outside the United States. The night ended with the girls dancing and the boys flirting. Unfortunately, this was the usual course of our nights out, and happened more times than I care to mention.

The Backstreet Boys were so busy that they would rarely double-date. There are a few occasions I remember when a few of us would go out together. Kevin's girlfriend Kristen was around during family gatherings. Brian's father and Kevin's mother are brother and sister and are very close. Kristen is one of the sweetest, most beautiful people I've ever met. Kevin was always at his best when she was by his side. Marissa, Alex's girlfriend at the time, was on tour with the band the same time I was. She was always a lot of fun. The four of us went to the New Edition reunion tour and had a great time. Howie's last girlfriend was Sabina. He met her in Germany, where she lived and danced for a living. When Sabina came out on tour, she would show me around to all the local spots. She was full of life and very sincere. All the girlfriends I met were so much fun, and I will never forget the experiences I shared with them. The girlfriends of the Boys were normal people just like you and me.

[29] Are any of the Backstreet Boys virgins?

This is a very personal question, but still one that is frequently asked. Honestly, I don't know about four out of the five guys. Of course, having thousands of girls throwing themselves at you night after night must be hard to resist. I'm sure temptation can have its way with you if you aren't careful. But I've watched the Backstreet Boys for four years and truly believe that they like a girl to save herself until the time is right.

> "Thousands of girls throwing themselves at you night after night must be hard to resist . . ."
>
> ♥

As for Brian, I could answer this question, but what fun would that be? I'd rather just leave that to your imagination. I would like to say that there is nothing wrong with waiting until you're married. You might be surprised how much respect you can gain!

[30] What do Brian and the Backstreet Boys like most about fans? What do they hate about them?

Imagine having people everywhere wanting a piece of you—wanting a piece of your clothing, your hair, your skin, anything. Sure, it can be fun, being so popular and having so many people want to catch a glimpse of you. But I've seen it turn dangerous. A mob scene can be scary, not only for the Backstreet Boys but for the fans. One time the Boys made an appearance at a school. The band had hired security, but they weren't prepared to handle the size of crowd that showed up. The situation quickly got out of control. The Backstreet Boys couldn't make it back to the bus, and I immediately knew they were in trouble. Brian was trying to move through the crowd toward the bus. He was wearing a new jacket he'd bought that had a hood. As fans were grabbing for a piece of the jacket, some of them pulled at the hood and threw Brian to the ground. The fans were swarming around Brian, and he almost got trampled. He was able to slip away, but the situation was so intense the hood to the jacket got ripped off in the process.

At one time or another, all of the Boys have felt threatened or invaded by their fans. That doesn't mean they don't love each and every one of you, it's just that sometimes things can get out of hand. One time Howie got stuck on the ground underneath a crowd and couldn't get up. Another time Alex was running away from a rushing crowd and his foot was run over by a limo. It can get scary. And I know the Boys are not only worried about their own safety, but their fans' safety too.

> *"A mob scene can be scary . . ."*
>
> ♥

Of course—and the boys know this—if all their fans didn't love them so much, they wouldn't be where they are today. It's kind of a double-edged sword. The band loves having all their fans chase after them, but at the same time they want everything to be kept cool and safe. They always like a crazy crowd, one that knows every word to their music. But there is nothing fun about getting hurt.

One time when the Backstreet Boys were performing at an exceptionally large venue in Canada, they were taken back by the fans. Before the show started the Boys thought there wasn't a way they could fill the entire venue. When the lights went down for the concert to begin, the fans went wild; the boys had never heard such a roar. When the show began they noticed that there wasn't an empty seat in the entire venue, the fans had sold the show out. The Boys were touched by their loyalty and how the audience knew every single word to every song. After the concert the Backstreet Boys were on an amazing high, all thanks to the fans. Knowing that the fans are happy and that their music touches others is the thing the Boys like most about their fans.

[31] Do the Backstreet Boys lip-sync in concert?

The tracks that are heard on the CDs, you have at home have been dubbed, redubbed, mastered, and, in short, made perfect for your listening pleasure. To get the same quality in concert, some of the vocals must be laid into the concert track. This basically means that different vocals you hear have been prerecorded and are playing along in the background with the music. The Backstreet Boys are not the only group that does this. It is a trick of the trade, but it doesn't mean that they aren't singing when they're up onstage. It only means that some of the voices you hear have already been recorded. When the Boys are breaking out into their choreographed moves, it's hard for them to keep up with all the vocals, so the tracks are also often used as a backup. Don't worry—the concerts are live, and the Backstreet Boys are truly belting out their songs. The Boys even have microphones that work backstage, so if they get caught in a wardrobe change, they can still make their singing cue.

> *"It is a trick of the trade. . . ."*
>
> ♥

There were many times I heard the Boys sing live with no microphones; sometimes it was even first thing in the morning. The Backstreet Boys almost always sounded nothing short of perfect. In the beginning of their careers, there were a few flaws that needed to be worked out, but now I think they have perfected their art. Wouldn't you say so?

[32] How do the Backstreet Boys feel about all the other boy groups that are popular right now?

The Backstreet Boys definitely realize how fortunate they are to be where they are. They've worked hard and have definitely had some breaks along the way. A lot of other bands, like 'N Sync, have gotten their share of breaks too. It's no coincidence that so many boy bands popped up at the same time. Just think about the similarities: five cute boys, great harmonies—and many of them have the same originating management. So of course there is some competition among the groups. The same management that started the Backstreet Boys and 'N Sync created a rivalry simply by bringing both bands out at the same time.

> *"I don't know if 'N Sync was actually trying to steal their fans away or not . . . "*
>
> ❤

For the most part, each group has such a hectic schedule that there is no time to think about the competition. But I do remember one interesting encounter the Backstreet Boys had with another boy group. I was touring with the band in Europe when we crossed paths with 'N Sync. We were leaving a hotel as 'N Sync was arriving. 'N Sync was fairly new at the time and didn't have as many fans. In Europe, fans were just crazy about the Backstreet Boys and would camp out at hotels just to get a glimpse of the band. It was a mob scene. The Backstreet Boys thought that 'N Sync might have planned to be crossing paths with them at the same hotel just to attract some of their fans away from them. I don't know if 'N Sync was actually trying to steal fans, but it really doesn't matter. There are plenty of boys out there for all of us to listen to and love.

'N Sync and the Backstreet Boys have had other chance meetings, and even a few planned ones. All in all, their encounters have gone well. They really do have a good relationship. They're competitive in a friendly and positive way.

Just like the saying goes, what goes around comes around. 'N Sync experienced some of the same competition about a year later. There's a new group called C-Note and this group was scheduled for some appearances at the same time as 'N Sync. 'N Sync had already established a fan base at this time and C-Note got to reap the benefits. Much like what happened with the Backstreet Boys and 'N Sync earlier. One of the members of C-Note named Raul told me that a few of the members of 'N Sync said that the extra competition is a little rough at times, but they would never want to treat a new group the way they had been treated by the Backstreet Boys. 'N Sync felt that if C-Note were to gain fans because of their popularity, then so be it, there's enough room in the entertainment business for more than one group to be popular. 'N Sync is very easygoing and although I don't know them personally, they seem to be a lot of fun and very sweet.

[33] What is Brian's biggest secret?

FUN FACTS!

Did you know that Brian is such a mamma's boy that his mom has been known to cut his steak for him? How sweet!

It's no big secret that Brian absolutely adores his mother. But not everyone knows just how much. More than any other guy I've met, Brian is a mama's boy. They are very close, which is so sweet.

> "When the steak came, something really interesting happened . . . "
>
> ♥

One experience with Brian and his mother really sticks out. Brian and I got our families together in Orlando. We decided to take them out for a steak dinner. Brian loves a good steak every once in a while. The dinner started off very nicely. I enjoyed spending time with Brian's parents, and our families got along fine. Brian has the nicest parents. But when the steak came, something really interesting happened. When we received our entrees, I was shocked to see Brian pass his plate over to his mother. She took his plate very naturally and put it and all his food in front of her. Then she began cutting up Brian's steak! I almost lost it. This was obviously something she had done for him since he was a young boy. He treated the whole thing very naturally and didn't mind a bit. I guess even a heartthrob never outgrows some things. When Brian's mom isn't around, maybe you can cut up his steak!

[34] How do the Backstreet Boys celebrate their birthdays?

All the Boys like to celebrate their birthdays in different ways. It varies from year to year, depending on the band's schedule. Sometimes they have to perform on one of their birthdays. None of them likes this, of course, but it's part of the business. Don't worry, though—the Boys always allow plenty of free time for fun.

> *"We danced and laughed all night . . . "*
>
> ♥

The birthday of Brian's I remember most was his twenty-second. We started the celebration in the afternoon and continued late into the night. We began the day at a go-cart track, where the Backstreet Boys and about fifty of their guests and friends raced each other until we simply couldn't race anymore. We then moved the party to a downtown dance club that the tour manager had rented. A few very resourceful fans crashed the party, but nothing serious happened, just good clean fun. We danced and laughed all night. I remember Alex out on the dance floor boogieing until he dropped. What a dancer! Even the normally dance-shy Brian got into the mix.

When we couldn't dance another step, everybody piled onto the bus and headed back to the hotel for some more late-night fun, which quickly ended with everyone retiring to their rooms for a good night's rest. It was definitely a night to remember. The tired, exhausted looks on our faces the next day told the whole story: we'd had a blast.

How can a fan meet the Backstreet Boys?

Unfortunately, I can't distribute the Backstreet Boys' addresses or phone numbers. Who knows, though—with these helpful hints you might be in the right place at the right time.

> *"The right place at the right time . . . "*
>
>

    The Backstreet Boys call Orlando, Florida, home. Brian has a home in Orlando. Nick and Brian have been spotted at local parks playing basketball. All of the Backstreet Boys enjoy shopping. We used to spend a lot of time at the Florida Mall and the West Oaks Mall. All of the boys, especially Alex, Kevin, and Howie, like to party in downtown Orlando at some of the local clubs. Some of their favorites are Baha Beach Club, Chillers, and Have a Nice Day. And as I've mentioned, Brian loves Red Lobster, so you never know if you'll spot him there. Just recently Brian was spotted ride-hopping at Universal Studios with his current girlfriend.

    Most of the Backstreet Boys' band lives in Orlando. A few of the members hang out or even play during their off-time at a local piano bar called Howl at the Moon. This piano bar is a lot of fun and I highly recommend you go if you can. Tim, the Backstreet Boys' keyboard player, likes to make an appearance at Howl at the Moon when he gets time off. Brian has gone to this piano bar to support his band. It's a party place to be.

But you don't have to go to Orlando to see the boys. They tour for so much of the year that they're probably on their way to your town right now.

Good luck with your search, girls!

FUN FACTS!

If you want to meet one of your favorite Backstreet Boys, your best bet is to come to Orlando and hang out at local basketball courts and malls.

[36] What was Brian's biggest surprise for you?

Brian had a big surprise for me during the Osceola High School homecoming parade in 1994. He can be so sweet. I was returning to Osceola to give my crown to the new homecoming queen. Going into the evening, I was so excited about the big event. Suddenly, we encountered a problem: I didn't have a car for the parade. Just before we had to leave, Brian came up with a plan that saved my day. He was able to borrow Lou Pearlman's light-blue convertible Rolls-Royce. He even helped out by driving the convertible during the parade.

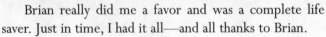

"Brian came up with a plan that saved my day . . . "

Brian really did me a favor and was a complete life saver. Just in time, I had it all—and all thanks to Brian.

Another time Brian surprised me . . . with himself. Brian got my dad to pick him up from the airport without me knowing. This was such a surprise because Brian wasn't due home for another week and had been gone for over a month. Brian surprised me at my high-school football game that I was cheering at. I was so happy to see him! Surprising me with himself was one of Brian's favorite things to do.

The sweetest thing Brian surprised me with was a tape with him singing a song to me. I was out dancing with my friend when out of nowhere Brian came out on the dance floor and handed me a tape. He said it was a special song for me and to wait to listen to it when I was alone. When no one was around I listened to the tape: It was Brian singing "Here And Now," a Luther Vandross song. Brian said he meant every word he was singing, I thought it was so sweet and a special surprise!

[37] How long did you tour with the Backstreet Boys? What was it like from day to day?

FUN FACTS!

The hardest part of being on tour with the Backstreet Boys is getting homesick. All of the boys were known to have enormously expensive phone bills!

Photo Credit: Bruce Wilson

Samantha
Stonebraker and
Brian Littrell.

Photo Credit: Teri Stonebraker

Samantha with Nick Carter's sister, B.J.

Hanging out with Alex before a video shoot.

*O*sceola High School
Homecoming Queen
Samantha Stonebraker and
her escort, Brian Littrell.

*A*t the prom.

A prom night kiss.

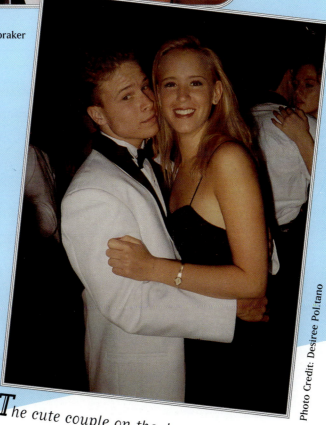

*T*he cute couple on the dance floor.

Smiling for the camera, Samantha and Brian were an adorable couple.

Photo Credit: Teri Stonebraker

Photo Credit: Samantha Stonebraker

The big day. High school graduation.

*B*rian, Samantha, Howie D., and a sorority sister of Samantha's at the Kappa Delta White Rose Formal, University of Central Florida.

A tender moment together.

*B*rian Littrell, caught off guard while getting ready for another long day as teen idol.

Photo Credit: Samantha Stonebraker

Photo Credit: Samantha Stonebraker

*B*rian with his car, the "Bleeding Banana."

Photo Credit: Samantha Stonebraker

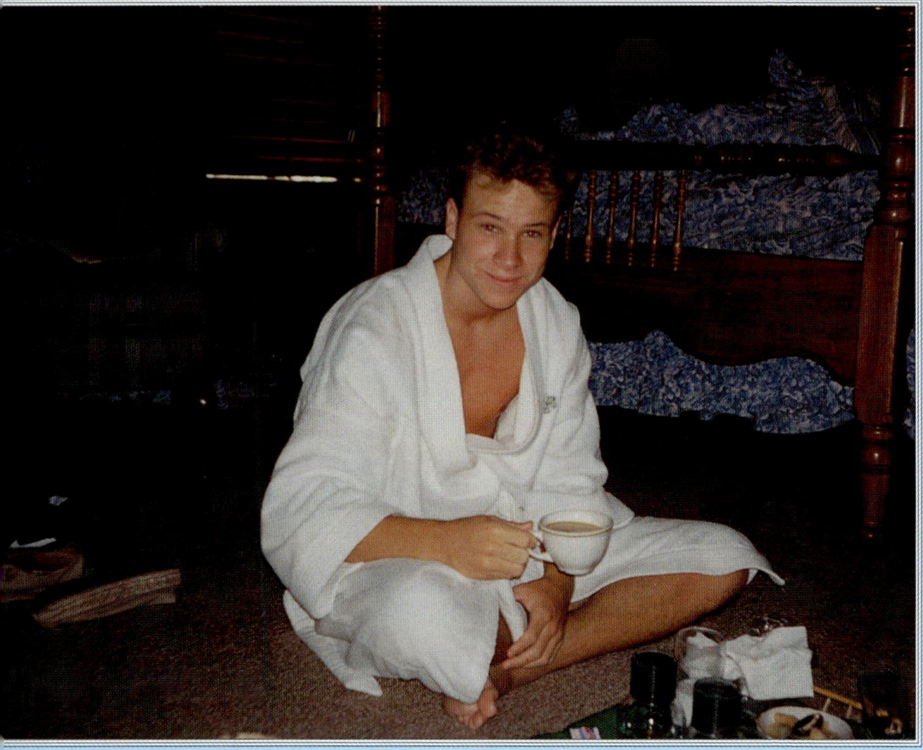

*The fine
physique of
Brian Littrell.*

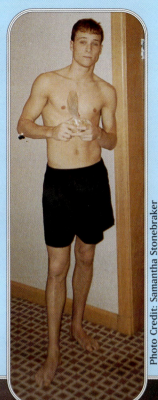

The Backstreet Boys.

*B*rian, Howie, A.J., and Kevin pose with a bodyguard.

A funny moment with the Boys.

*B*rian and the rest of the Backstreet Boys doing what they do best . . . performing.

*T*he boys at a "Teen People" party.

*O*n the beach with Brian.

*W*ith his proud
parents.

*B*rian Littrell,
the graduate.

*M*ore candid shots.

Wouldn't you love to be the girlfriend of one of these guys?

Life on the road is extremely difficult to get used to. I traveled with the Boys off and on for over a year. For a few months straight I was with the Backstreet Boys during their European tour. Every day begins and ends in a different city with a different feel. Homesickness is common on the road, as any of the Boys will attest. We typically started off the day with a five A.M. wake-up call. The band then would go through hours of bus travel, interviews, and photo shoots. Everyone builds up all this energy during the day, because you're sitting around so much. The concert itself is the perfect release for all the built-up energy. After the concert, it all starts over again. It was always a sure bet that we would be traveling to a new hotel in a new city, just to get there in time to repeat the hectic schedule again the next day.

> *"A different city with a different feel . . . "*
>
> ♥

I know it sounds like too much to handle, but it's not all bad. I mean, seeing a new city every day, being with your good friends, and partying every night has its perks, right? But it can get lonely, and a good phone call home is nice, even if it doesn't always do the trick.

You might wonder why the Backstreet Boys and other bands take these tours day in and day out. Well, the answer is simple: they do it for the fans and the music. The fans' energy and the Boys' love of music are what it's all about.

[38] What kind of clothes do Brian and the other Backstreet Boys like their girlfriends to wear?

I get this question a lot, because girls want to know how to attract or impress the Backstreet Boys. As you know, all of the band members like different styles of clothing, and the same can be said about what they like girls to wear. Of course, people dress according to their lifestyles. Alex is very alternative, so he likes his girlfriends to be creative with their wardrobe. Alex's style can be over-the-top, which a lot of people can't pull off and still look good. You would have to be one of those girls that could pull off this unique style to attract Alex. Kevin has always loved style. He's the most stylish of the group. His girlfriend Kristen is from New York and has always had a classy but cutting-edge look. Kristen has always been a style setter, not a style follower. Howie has never been tied down to one particular style. His girlfriends dress in an array of outfits ranging from long dresses to short shorts. Howie's freeness to style matches his relaxed personality. I do have to mention that Howie's girlfriend, Sabina, had a very sexy wardrobe and Howie loved it. Nick and Brian always like their girlfriends in cute, fresh, and hip styles. Tommy Jeans were always a favorite. They like revealing outfits, but not too much exposure. Brian's favorite body part is the legs so he always enjoyed seeing me in a skirt. He would often buy cute sundresses for me so he could get a peek at my legs.

> "They like revealing outfits, but not too much exposure . . ."
>
> ❤

Here's a hot tip: Brian loves for his girls to wear his clothes. So if you dress like Brian, he'll likely be attracted to what you're wearing. Brian always did tell me that he thought I was my prettiest first thing in the morning, with no makeup on and wearing baggy flannels.

[39] Do you wish you could have dated one of the other the Backstreet Boys? How did the other members treat their girlfriends?

That's a tough question, since I only dated Brian. While I saw the way the other boys treated their girlfriends, I don't know how they would have treated me.

> *"Kevin is very sexy . . . "*
>
> ♥

I've always thought that Kevin is very sexy. He does have a tendency to be a little meticulous, though. For example, Kevin was known for wanting all the choreography to look perfect onstage. During rehearsals, Kevin was the member that encouraged the Boys to repeat moves over and over until they were perfect. I would be afraid to be his girlfriend because I'd feel I'd have to be perfect all the time. That's not me. Nick is a complete sweetheart. I always looked at him like a little brother, though, so it's hard to be attracted to him. Nick has a good heart and deserves someone who will truly love him for who he is. He's an adorable young man. A. J. has a great style and loves to just have fun. The thing I liked most about Alex is his love for dancing: there's nothing hotter to me than a guy who can tear it up on the dance floor. Howie is the most romantic of the group. He treats his girlfriends extremely well, with plenty of presents and candlelit dinners.

They are all very sweet, very different guys, and I wouldn't trade the time that I shared with any of them for the world. With all that said, however, I've never wished that I'd dated anyone other than Brian. One is enough and all I could handle! From flying their girlfriends in to see them when they are in some foreign place to romantic sunset walks on the beach, the Boys are some very classy guys. Who would your dream date be with, and what would you do?

[40] What is the most outrageous thing you ever saw a fan do?

There is one story that even I have a hard time believing, and I lived through it. It's what I like to call the stowaway story. You might even have heard one of the Backstreet Boys mention it before, but let me fill you in on the complete story. I was traveling with the Boys while they were on tour in Europe. This particular day we had to load the bus in the middle of the night to travel to the next city. This was not uncommon at all. The Backstreet Boys' tour schedule was so demanding that a hotel bed was sometimes traded for a bunk on the tour bus, just so we could arrive at the next scheduled show on time. We had a three A.M. wake-up call because we had to get on the bus within thirty minutes. Everything seemed normal; Nick, Alex, Brian, Howie, Kevin, and their guests were all accounted for and on the bus. Little did we know as we climbed into our bunks that there were a few uninvited passengers in the tour bus's stowaway luggage compartment!

> "While we were tucked away contentedly in our bunks, things got crazy . . ."

All I can remember is the bus stopping midway through our trip. There was a lot of commotion, and Johnny Wright, the manager at the time, yelled for Randy, the security guard. I was kind of half asleep and must have drifted back off.

That morning, when we made it safely to the next show, Johnny told us the whole story. While we were tucked away contentedly in our bunks, things got crazy. No one knew how, but two Backstreet Boys fans had found a way to sneak onto the tour bus, maybe while luggage was being loaded. Regardless, they got on and hid in the stow-away compartment until Johnny discovered them as he was shifting positions in his bunk. Johnny realized he had grabbed a leg and followed it up to the owner. It was crazy! One of the girls didn't even have shoes on. The girls were dropped off, and the Boys' manager forced them to call their parents to come get them. Those girls really went to some extreme measures to get closer to the Backstreet Boys. The whole episode really scared and freaked everyone out. If you're trying to think of ways to meet the Backstreet Boys, count this one out! You may meet them, but you'll never get them to like you this way.

FUN FACTS!

The most outrageous thing a fan ever did in front of me was sneak onto the Backstreet Boys tour bus and hide in the stowaway. We all found this to be crazy. I wouldn't recommend a fan try this.

How can a fan break into the music business?

The first step to breaking into the music business is to truly love music. This journey is a long and drawn-out process, and around every corner is someone trying to knock you down. For every person who wants you to succeed, there are fifty trying to ruin you. A love of music is essential if you want to succeed. I watched five down-home boys turn into superstars. But the Backstreet Boys were told from the beginning that they were entering show *business*, not the show family. As cold as it seems, that's the reality. Don't get me wrong—the Boys did act like family, but they realized that big business was running the show. Their true love for music makes them stronger and separates them from a lot of imitators who just don't make the grade. Brian has this love of music in him. It's obvious just from the emotion in his voice.

> "The Boys did act like family, but realized that big business was running the show . . ."
>
> ❤

Another key to breaking into the business is practice. For some, singing comes easier than for others. For example, Howie has taken voice lessons since he was young, but Brian was never professionally trained until he joined the

Backstreet Boys. The way you go about practicing is up to you, but it must be a part of your life. Brian hadn't had formal vocal instruction, but he'd practiced on his own every chance he got. Through family, church, and school, Brian was able to master his vocal instrument.

Success can also be determined by just being at the right place at the right time. I know numerous talented artists who are unemployed. Sometimes it's just the luck of the draw, being what they're looking for at that moment. Regardless, stay educated. One thing I remember most about Brian is how he wished he could have gone to college. You can be on top of the charts one day and a nobody the next. Audiences can be fickle things. Your education is the one thing that can never be taken away from you! Beyond that, work hard, be yourself, and remember where you come from.

[42]

Did you and Brian ever have a pet together?

Brian's first pet was a cat named Missy. Brian brought Missy to his family's home. Missy is a very temperamental cat. I can remember her knocking things over on purpose to get people's attention. Brian's mom used to tease him about moving to Florida and leaving his cat behind. Brian was the only person Missy really loved. Missy really loved Brian when he was working at Long John Silver's in high school. He would come home with a fishy smell and that cat would love on him for hours.

> *"Missy the cat really loved Brian when he was working at Long John Silver's . . . "*
>
>

Since Brian spent most of his time at my family's home while we were dating, he considered our family dog, Beauty, to be his own. I can remember him writing about her in interviews for magazines. Beauty is a female collie, who has been a member of the Stonebraker family for years. She's like one of the kids. Beauty was such a big part of his life at one time that many of you may know of her from articles on Brian. The confusion over who actually owned Beauty still floats around in books I've read recently. Now you know the real story behind Brian's pet collie.

After Brian and I broke up, we both added new animals to our lives. He got a Chihuahua while I got a light-yellow Lab. These are such different breeds of dogs, but they both really fit out personalities. I know Brian is very proud of his Tyke. He takes him everywhere he can, usually in an outfit that matches that of his current girlfriend. I can somewhat identify with this behavior. I don't dress my Lab up for award shows, like Brian does, but he does goes running, fishing, and even out on the golf course or the beach with me and my boyfriend. Stoney is the name of my Lab, given to me by my boyfriend Stephen as a birthday gift. He is only nine months old. Stephen and I came up with the name Stoney from my last name. I can't explain the energy Stoney has. He can outrun or outswim anyone.

Although we never bought a pet together, there have been many animals in our lives at the same time. More than one animal has claimed Brian's heart. Now you know the stories behind Missy the cat, Beauty the collie, and Tyke the Chihuahua.

FUN FACTS!

Brian loves to dress his Chihuahua like himself for award shows. Talk about a doggie with style!

[43]

What music inspired Brian and the Boys?

It's no secret how how much Brian loves music. When you're an artist, it's important to always be expanding your musical knowledge, and I always encouraged Brian to do so. I'm sure you know Brian loves rhythm-and-blues, but did you know that one of his musical influences is James Taylor? Nick is truly inspired by classic rock bands like Journey. Nick has told me before that if he could, he would write and sing that type of music. Alex didn't always sing best-selling tunes. In fact, in high school he was best known for oldies and the classics. The Backstreet Boys' influences really come from a lot of different places.

"From Journey to Jimmy Buffett . . ."

♥

I'll never forget taking Brian to the Eagles' "Hell Freezes Over" tour. Brian and I went with my family and had excellent seats. The Eagles' talent really captivated Brian. The performance, the music, and the longevity of the band truly inspired him. Brian was so excited that he had to leave the concert briefly to call his mom and share his excitement with her.

From Journey to Jimmy Buffett, the Backstreet Boys know their music. These influences have inspired the boys to chart-topping status. Music is the Backstreet Boys' life, and they know how to live it.

[44] Do any of the Backstreet Boys play an instrument?

All of the Backstreet Boys are masters of one instrument; the voice. Some of the boys are multitalented and have the ability to play other instruments. As long as the Backstreet Boys have the desire to conquer something new, they will. They progress more and more every day musically, and if playing a particular instrument is the next step, they will take it.

> *"At all hours of the night I would hear Kevin having a jam session with his side-kick Keith, a.k.a. Trey D . . . "*
>
>

For as long as I've known him, Kevin has played the piano. I remember going to his apartment when he lived with Brian and seeing his keyboard and equipment set up in the corner. At all hours of the night I would hear Kevin having a jam session with his best friend Keith, a.k.a. Trey D. Nick has always enjoyed playing the drums. He used to tease the Backstreet Boys' drum player, Tim, saying that if Tim gave him too many drum lessons, he would take his job. The entire backup band was helpful when it came to teaching the Boys different instruments. When the Boys filmed "Quit Playing Games," Howie didn't know how to play the guitar but wanted to learn. Lenny, the guitar player for the boys at the time, taught Howie a few chords so he could play for the video. Brian really became interested in playing the guitar while writing "That's What She Said." He discovered that music was just as important as lyrics. Lenny began coaching him. Any free second Brian had, he was trying to learn. One day, to show how much Brian meant to him, Kevin gave Brian his father's guitar. Brian loves that guitar because of the sentimental value it holds.

The Backstreet Boys are talented and take music seriously. They always enjoy expanding their musical knowledge.

[45] What was your relationship with the parents of the Backstreet Boys like?

I never had a confrontation with any of the Backstreet Boys' parents. In fact, I enjoyed the company of all of them and bonded closely with some—especially Nick's mom, Jane. Jane Carter is simply awesome. She's pretty, fun, and intelligent. It is plain to see how much she cares for her family. Jane and I got closer out on tour with the Boys. It helped that Brian and Nick were so close. It was hard to know whom you could trust while surrounded by businessmen and -women, so as soon as we realized we could trust each other, we became a team.

> *"Jane Carter is simply awesome . . . "*
>
>

There was one time we really lived it up. The Backstreet Boys had a day engagement at a different location than their concert that night. So they flew to their gig while Jane and her youngest son, Aaron, and I took the tour bus to the hotel. We were in Europe, in a place where the weather is usually cloudy and on the cool side. To our surprise, however, it was beautiful that day when we arrived at the hotel—around seventy degrees and sunny. It took only seconds for the Florida girls in Jane and me to come out. We didn't need to say anything; we just knew to get on our bathing suits and meet by the pool ASAP. So we did just that. Jane and I lay by the pool all day while Aaron romped around on the deck. It was so great. We really bonded.

When it was time to go to the show, we dressed up together. Jane is a fabulous dresser. I had never been around a mom cool enough that you would want to wear her wardrobe. After a day in the sun, we were ready for a night out. We only got as far as the Backstreet Boys' show, but we made our own fun!

 **[46]** Did you ever hear Brian sing in church?

Brian was always ready to go to church with my family on Sundays. Brian was essentially a member of my family when we dated. We went to church in Winter Garden because we fell in love with Father Jim, the priest at the church. It's hard to describe how Father Jim Radebaugh touched our lives, but he did, in so many ways. The way Father Jim would preach was unique. He would incorporate cute and interesting personal stories to go along with the sermons. This gave us a feeling that we were being preached to, not preached at. Father Jim encouraged us to think for ourselves and not just to settle for what we heard. Brian found Father Jim very special, and my family is still inspired by his words.

> "When it came time to sing, Brian was the first one to hit a tune . . . "
>
> ♥

When it came time to sing, Brian was the first one to hit a tune. Brian loved to express his thanks through song. He was always on-key and loved to throw in a harmony at the end of a hymn. Even though Brian normally worshiped at a Baptist church, he found that Father Jim's preaching went beyond denomination. Brian used to playfully race us to Father Jim at the end of the sermon, so he could be the first to receive a "Father Jim hug."

Just in the last year, Father Jim has found out he was dying of cancer. He passed away on September 4, 1999, but I know his memory and spiritual inspiration never will. Father Jim will remain in our hearts forever.

Did any of the Backstreet Boys break their girl-friends' hearts?

Every couple has arguments—a certain amount is normal. It would be silly to think that the Backstreet Boys aren't human enough to break someone's heart or even to have their hearts broken. I've seen all the boys argue with their girlfriends at one time or another. Brian and I definitely knew how to push each other's buttons. It's something you learn the longer you're with someone. This isn't so bad, I guess; it's just something people do to get what they want.

> *"Late one night, Brian was alone with a lady friend in his hotel room for hours . . ."*
>
> ♥

Howie is the most romantic Backstreet Boy. His girlfriend at the time I was seeing Brian was Sabina. Since Sabina lived in Germany and Howie was based in Orlando, they would go for months without seeing each other. This led to them missing each other, which caused a lot of frustration. But they couldn't stand to be apart. While I don't know if they're still dating, they sure had a lot of passion back then. If Howie is single, girls, and you're looking for romance, he's the one to snatch up.

Once I found out that late one night, Brian was alone with a lady friend in his hotel room for hours—well into the early morning. I was shocked. What was he doing or thinking? One thing about the Boys is that they don't get away with much. Someone usually sees them when they're up to no good. If one girlfriend was out on the road with the boys, she would keep an eye on the other boys for their girlfriends. I still don't know what happened in Brian's room that night, and I probably never will. All I know is what Brian told me: "Nothing happened." Ultimately I had to trust Brian.

Sometimes in relationships you will get your heart broken. Sometimes things can be mended—and sometimes it can tear a relationship apart forever.

[48] Why did you write this book?

I wrote this book for many reasons. First of all, I wrote it for my family, specifically my brothers, Steven and John, and my sister, Mari. My breakup with Brian was like a divorce. We had a joint bank account and even had bought a car together. My parents had taken Brian in as one of their own children. Since Brian lived at my family's home, my siblings grew very close to him and looked to him as an older brother. My breakup with Brian was intensified by the fact that he was a Backstreet Boy. It's hard to forget about someone when everywhere you turn, you see him on television, T-shirts, and album covers. After our breakup my siblings were left with a lot of confusion, which I hope this book will help to clarify, so they can put an end to that chapter of their lives.

> *"There is life after a breakup, even if it is with one of the Backstreet Boys . . ."*
>
>

Another reason is that I wrote it for you, the reader. Not only do I want you to get a firsthand, exclusive insight into the Backstreet Boys, but I also I want you to realize that there is life after a breakup, even if it is with one of the Backstreet Boys. I don't regret my past or my relationship with Brian. I actually cherish it, because it has made me the woman I am today. In life you have to take the good with the bad. To be successful, you keep the good close to your heart and utilize the bad as a learning tool. It wasn't until after I broke up with Brian that I gained the drive to continue and finish my college education. Now I am a graduate of the University of Central Florida with a degree in communicative disorders.

When you're hurt or down for whatever reason, anyone can choose to mope and be depressed. It takes a winner to turn the bad times into good. The energy that you spend being depressed about something or *someone* can be used more wisely on yourself. Take that energy and create a better you. Find a hobby or educate yourself. The lesson to be learned is to truly love *you*. I'm not claiming to have all the answers; I simply know what I've experienced in my own life.

Always remember that you are beautiful. The beauty you have on the inside with your personality and laughter will radiate outward. This is what makes one truly beautiful. Take each day and enjoy the dance of life.

[49] Did Brian go to college with you?

Brian did not go to college, but he always wished he had. Because of the Backstreet Boys' schedule, they had little time to do much else than work. Brian did try to be a part of my college life whenever possible. He knew he was missing out on a lot, academically and socially. It's funny how school can sometimes seem like a bore, but when it's taken away, you realize how important it is. I decided to go to the University of Central Florida so I would be close to Brian and we wouldn't have to break up after high school—long-distance relationships are always harder. But I would never recommend someone make a college choice the way I did! While I was living on the college campus, Brian decided to move into my parents' house. My parents invited him into their home and treated him like he was one of the kids. Since I had moved out, there was extra room, and Brian loved being part of the family. It was a great setup. I lived on campus during the week, and on weekends I drove an hour to my parents' house to see the family, which now included Brian.

> "B-Rok would belt "I Just Called to Say I Love You" so the whole sorority house could hear . . . "
>
> ♥

I joined a sorority called Kappa Delta as soon as I started school. This was a big change for me. It was the first time I lived outside of my parents' home. I missed my brothers and sister, but Brian kept me company whenever possible. My college roommate teases me to this day about Brian calling our answering machine and singing random songs on it. B-Rok would belt "I Just Called to Say I Love You" so the whole sorority house could hear. Brian was known for leaving love notes and flowers for me while I was in class. The most fun we had was when Brian wasn't a Backstreet Boy; he was just a normal guy hanging with me and my college friends.

One time when Brian was in town, he went with my sorority on a bus ride to a football game. Brian was so excited. We had a blast. The fraternity that was on the bus with us was joking with Brian and singing "We've Got It Goin' On." Brian loved it. When we got to the game, we cheered on the UCF Knights. Brian felt like he was a true Knight for a day, and he didn't want to go home. But the best time we had was when we went to Kappa Delta's White Rose Formal. Brian was able to bring along one of his fellow group members—Howie. Brian and I set Howie up with one of my sorority sisters, named Christy. We had so much fun.

The night of the White Rose Formal was a blast. Since I was a member of Kappa Delta, this was a big night for us. We started the night at one of my sorority sisters' apartments. About six of my sisters and their dates were at the apartment. When it came time to leave for the formal, we were one date short: Howie was running late, which was not unusual for him at the time. Finally, he showed up with just about fifteen minutes to spare. Christy was so relieved! When Brian asked him why he took so long, Howie told him that he was nervous and couldn't decide what to wear. Even the Backstreet Boys get predate jitters.

There was one bad moment to the evening. Some of the fraternity boys attending the formal made fun of Brian for being so short. Brian took the comment lightly and laughed it off. Brian was the bigger man because he didn't sink to their insulting level. The fraternity boys were really just jealous of Brian's success and trying to knock him down a notch.

When we arrived at the formal, we were ready for a good time. Once I got Brian out on the dance floor, he wouldn't stop—he danced the night away. Brian was stealing the show out on the dance floor. This was so out of character for Brian, no one could believe it! I think he enjoyed the night so much because he was able to be himself.

One funny story about Howie and his date, Christy. Howie was so much shorter than Christy that she wouldn't wear her high heels. It was so cute. She was barefoot while they were slow dancing. The last thing Christy wanted was for Howie to feel uncomfortable, so she went to all measures to make him feel taller.

We ended the night with lots of laughs and memories. Howie said he would be a blind date anytime. We all agreed it was a wonderful night!

Brian had some of the best times pretending he was a college student. Maybe furthering your education isn't so boring after all.

[50] How did your four-year relationship with Brian come to an end?

When two people grow and mature, they can either grow apart or grow together. By the end of our relationship, Brian and I had begun to grow apart. We were becoming very different people and wanting different things out of life.

> "The next thing I knew I was being rushed out of the concert arena on a stretcher and into an ambulance . . . "

There was one major incident that started the rift between us. I was on tour with the Backstreet Boys in Europe. I believe we were somewhere in the middle of Germany. The Backstreet Boys were just a couple of weeks short of ending their summer tour. After dinner one night, I began to get intense stomach pains. When I got back to the hotel with Brian, I began to vomit everywhere. My sickness and pain lasted all night. Five days later I was still sick and still had stomach pains. By this point I could barely move and was restricted to the tour bus while the boys were performing. Going without food and not being able to keep water down without vomiting for *five* days is extremely dangerous. Brian would bring me bread and water while I was bedridden on the tour bus. Sounds glamorous, doesn't it!

You may be wondering why I didn't go to the hospital. Well, being stranded in the middle of a foreign country and not speaking the local language, on top of being severely ill, has its disadvantages. I was so weak that I needed someone to take charge and see that I was taken to the hospital. For fours days no one did, because the tour manager was worried that if I was seen going to the hospital, it might leak to the press that the Backstreet Boys had girlfriends— or worse, I could delay their tour schedule by being in the hospital. (Luckily for them, the Backstreet Boys don't have this tour manager any longer.)

Brian at this point could see that I wasn't recovering from this mysterious sickness, so on the fifth day he made arrangements for me to fly back to the States. Brian told the tour manager that the airline must be alerted that I was ill so they would take special care of me. Once again the tour manager intervened by saying that I didn't deserve such "princess treatment." Before I could make it to the flight, my health took a turn for the worse. My stomach ached to the point that I could no longer move. I must have been turning gray, because Angie, the Boys' makeup artist, took one look at me and demanded I be taken to the hospital.

The Backstreet Boys were performing onstage, so I couldn't get to Brian to tell him I was being taken to the hospital. Since Angie was working, the caterer agreed to go with me to the hospital. This worked out well, because she could speak both English and German and would act as my translator. The next thing I knew I was being rushed out of the concert arena on a stretcher and into an ambulance. I was so scared—everyone was speaking a language I couldn't understand and I was in such pain. I arrived at the hospital and in a matter of minutes the doctors found stones in my gall bladder. The mystery of my pains was solved. I had been having gall bladder attacks for five entire days. I took the next available flight home to Orlando and had my gall bladder removed shortly thereafter.

Because Brian didn't immediately take me to the hospital, missing an appearance if necessary, this made me lose faith in our relationship. The truth? I felt Brian let me down. We didn't break up immediately, but things were never the same. A few months later we ended the relationship.

It has taken a while, but not only have I gotten over this experience, I've grown from it. Brian and I were so young when we started dating. As we matured, we grew apart. I started to realize that the type of entertainment business I was experiencing wasn't for me. I wanted to continue my education and graduate from college. After we broke up, I did just that. Today, I am healthier and happier than ever. It did take a while, but I learned to trust again and am in love with an incredible man. Brian too has moved on and is involved with an older woman. I learned a lot from my breakup with Brian, and it has helped my current relationship to be more productive and healthy. You can move on from relationships and become more empowered than you ever thought possible.

WHAT YOU WANNA KNOW Sweepstakes
No Purchase Necessary
This Sweepstakes has not been authorized or endorsed by the Backstreet Boys.

Enter to Win:

• A photo signed by all five Backstreet Boys
• Brian Littrell's European Tour Jacket
• Backstreet Boys' Gold Album for "I'll Never Break Your Heart"

OFFICIAL ENTRY FORM

Enter to win (check one item per Sweepstakes entry):

____ A photo signed by all five Backstreet Boys
____ Brian Littrell's European Tour Jacket
____ Backstreet Boys' Gold Album for "I'll Never Break Your Heart"

Mail to:
WHAT YOU WANNA KNOW Sweepstakes
St. Martin's Press
Attn: JV
175 5th Avenue
Suite 1615
New York, NY 10010-7848

Name: _____
Address :_____
City/State/Zip:_____
Phone (day): _____ Phone (night): _____
Email: _____

See next page for Official Rules. No purchase necessary. Void in the province of Quebec, Puerto Rico and wherever else prohibited by law. Entries must be postmarked no later than February 7, 2000 and received no later than February 14, 2000.

OFFICIAL RULES

1. To Enter: Complete the Official Entry Form, stating which prize you want the entry to qualify for, and mail it to: *What You Wanna Know* Sweepstakes, c/o St. Martin's Press, 175 Fifth Avenue, Suite 1615, New York, NY 10010-7848, attention: JV, or send a postcard with your name and complete address and identifying the prize you want the entry to qualify for to the same address. Enter as many times as you want, but each entry must be mailed separately, and be sure to state on each entry what prize you are entering for. You can try for a different prize on each entry. To be eligible, entries must be postmarked no later than February 7, 2000 and received no later than February 14, 2000. Not responsible for lost, misdirected, mutilated, or late entries.

2. Random Drawing. There will be a separate drawing for each prize. Winners will be determined in random drawings to be held on or about March 1, 2000, from all eligible entries received. Odds of winning a prize in a drawing depend on the number of eligible entries received for that drawing. Potential winners will be notified by mail on or about March 22, 2000, and will be asked to execute and return an Affidavit of Eligibility/Release/Prize Acceptance Form within fourteen (14) days of attempted notification. Winners under the age of 18 will also be required to have a parent or legal guardian sign the form. Noncompliance within this time may result in disqualification and the selection of an alternate winner. Return of any prize/prize notification as undeliverable will result in disqualification and an alternate winner will be selected.

3. Prize and Approximate Retail Value: The prizes and approximate retail values are:

> A photo signed by all five Backstreet Boys—approximate retail value $300
> Brian Littrell's European Tour Jacket—approximate retail value $300
> Backstreet Boys' Gold Album for "I'll Never Break Your Heart"—approximate retail value $1,000

4. Eligibility. Open to U.S. and Canadian residents (excluding residents of the province of Quebec). Employees of St. Martin's Press, its parent, affiliates, and subsidiaries, its and their directors, managers, officers and agents, and their immediate families or those living in the same household, are ineligible to enter. Potential Canadian winners will be required to correctly answer a time-limited arithmetic-skill question by mail. Void in Puerto Rico and wherever else prohibited by law.

5. General Conditions: One prize per person. Winners are responsible for all federal, state and local taxes. No substitution or cash redemption of prizes permitted by winners. Prizes are not transferable. Acceptance of prize constitutes permission to use winner's name, photograph, and likeness for purposes of advertising and promotion without additional compensation or permission, unless prohibited by law.

6. All entries become the property of sponsor and will not be returned. By participating in this sweepstakes, entrants agree to be bound by these official rules and the decision of the judges, which are final in all respects.

7. For the name of the winners, available after March 22, 2000, send by May 1, 2000, a stamped, self-addressed envelope to Winner's List, *What You Wanna Know* Sweepstakes, St. Martin's Press, 175 Fifth Avenue, Suite 1615, New York, NY 10010-7848, attention: JV.